"I BELIEVE THAT EVERYTHING HAPPENS FOR A REASON. PEOPLE CHANGE SO THAT YOU CAN LEARN TO LET GO, THINGS GO WRONG SO THAT YOU CAN APPRECIATE THEM WHEN THEY'RE RIGHT, YOU BELIEVE LIES SO YOU EVENTUALLY LEARN TO TRUST NO ONE BUT YOURSELF, AND SOMETIMES GOOD THINGS FALL APART SO BETTER THINGS CAN FALL TOGETHER."

MARILYN MONROE

1926–1962

ABDO
Publishing Company

MARILYN MONROE

HOLLYWOOD ICON

BY LISA OWINGS

CREDITS

Published by ABDO Publishing Company, PO Box 398166, Minneapolis, MN 55439. Copyright © 2013 by Abdo Consulting Group, Inc. International copyrights reserved in all countries. No part of this book may be reproduced in any form without written permission from the publisher. The Essential Library™ is a trademark and logo of ABDO Publishing Company.

Printed in the United States of America, North Mankato, Minnesota
062012
092012

 THIS BOOK CONTAINS AT LEAST 10% RECYCLED MATERIALS.

Editor: Rebecca Felix
Series Designer: Becky Daum

Library of Congress Cataloging-in-Publication Data
Owings, Lisa.
  Marilyn Monroe : Hollywood icon / by Lisa Owings.
     p. cm. -- (Lives cut short)
  Includes bibliographical references and index.
  ISBN 978-1-61783-481-3
  1. Monroe, Marilyn, 1926-1962--Juvenile literature. 2. Motion picture actors and actresses--United States--Biography--Juvenile literature. I. Title.
  PN2287.M69O85 2012
  791.4302'8092--dc23
  [B]
                                        2012001291

TABLE OF CONTENTS

1

BETTER THAN BIRTHDAY CAKE

In the spring of 1962, Marilyn Monroe was perhaps more beautiful than she had ever been. At nearly 36 years old, she was trim, though still in possession of her signature curves. Her hair was white-blonde, and many noted the open and vulnerable character of the famous face it framed. Though beautiful, Monroe was also troubled during the last spring of her life. She had begun filming *Something's Got to Give*, produced by Twentieth Century Fox. She missed several days of filming, either too sick, too drug addled, or too

▸ MARILYN MONROE IN 1962

depressed to work, putting the film dangerously behind schedule. When she came back to work, she acted beautifully, but her mind seemed to be occupied with something else.

Just days after she returned to the set, Monroe went missing again. This time she was on her way to New York City, where she would sing "Happy Birthday" to the president of the United States at a gala in the huge Madison Square Garden arena. Fox had given her permission to go and then withdrew it after the unforeseen delays in filming. But Monroe was not about to let anyone stop her from performing for her president and her public. She ignored Fox's threats to fire her, daring the company to cut ties with its biggest star.

She had every detail of the performance planned, envisioning the shocking effect she would have on her audience. She had been secretly rehearsing a sexy, half-whispered version of "Happy Birthday," recording her voice and then playing it back until she achieved exactly the style she wanted. She had a dress made to fit her body so perfectly she looked almost nude in it, though she told the man in charge of the event she would wear something conservative. She was about to show the president and the world how powerful her sex appeal could be.

▲ MONROE SINGING "HAPPY BIRTHDAY" TO PRESIDENT KENNEDY ON MAY 19, 1962

HAPPY BIRTHDAY, MR. PRESIDENT

On May 19, 1962, the night of President John F. Kennedy's birthday gala, Monroe was late as usual. The designer of her dress had to sew her into it before the performance, making stitches up the sides. The dress was made of a delicate, sheer fabric the color of Monroe's skin. It was covered in shimmering beads, which glistened on what seemed to be her bare figure. Since she could barely walk in the fitted gown, Monroe had to be carried downstairs to the stage. She pulled on a fur wrap to keep the dress a secret just a little bit longer. Finally, Monroe was ready for the entrance of a lifetime.

Film actor Peter Lawford, friend to Monroe and brother-in-law to the president, gave Monroe a comedic introduction. Poking fun at her reputation for lateness, he said, "This lovely lady is not only [beautiful] but punctual." When he announced, "Mr. President, Marilyn Monroe," the spotlight gleamed on an empty stage. No Marilyn. He went on, "It truly may be said she needs no introduction. Let me just say, here she is." He gestured again to the empty stage, drawing laughter from the crowd. As Lawford proceeded with the introduction, Monroe stepped onto the stage behind him. Holding her wrap close, she shimmied up to the microphone. Lawford concluded, "Mr. President, the *late* Marilyn Monroe."[1] When Lawford took Monroe's wrap, revealing the dress, the crowd gasped.

Monroe herself felt a bit of stage fright. She later said in an interview for *Life* magazine, "There was like a hush over the whole place when I came on to sing 'Happy Birthday.' . . . I thought, 'Oh, my gosh, what if no sound comes out!'"[3] Monroe took a deep, shaky breath, seemingly comforted by her audience's cheers. And then her sound did come out—the carefully crafted sound that would be remembered for decades after her death—her sexy, intimate version of "Happy Birthday." While she sang, Monroe moved her hand seductively along the curves of her body. People were shocked by this bold act but could not deny the timelessness and allure of her beauty.

Monroe's Tardiness

Monroe was notoriously late for nearly everything. Though this trait frustrated friends and coworkers, they could not change her and usually had to work around her. Monroe took sleeping pills that often made it difficult for her to wake up in the morning. Use of sleeping pills and stimulants was an accepted practice at the time. Monroe was also a perfectionist and deeply insecure, leading her to spend hours perfecting her appearance or rehearsing her lines. In an interview published in *Life* magazine, Monroe stated she would rather be prepared than be on time. She said,

The main thing is, I do want to be prepared when I get there to give a good performance or whatever to the best of my ability. A lot of people can be there on time and do nothing. . . . [Clark] Gable said about me, "When she's there,

After Monroe finished her song, she invited everyone in the audience to join her in another round of "Happy Birthday." As they sang, two waiters brought out a giant tiered birthday cake as tall as the waiters and glowing in the flicker of many birthday candles. Then President Kennedy took the stage and joked, "Thank you. I can now retire from politics after having 'Happy Birthday' sung to me in such a sweet, wholesome way."[5] That night, Monroe seemed to be at the height of her power and fame. No one in attendance would have predicted that less than three months later, she would be gone.

A Myth

Monroe's performance for the president fueled rumors that the two were having an affair. Rumors such as these were part of Monroe's Hollywood life. Whether true or false, they were part of who she was, and she accepted that. She sometimes cultivated these rumors, creating a mythical character distinctly different from her true self that contributed to the mystique of her persona.

In the decades since Monroe's death, many rumors have proved false, and many truths have emerged. Though at times it seems no one can tell the difference between the character and the

▲ ALTHOUGH MANY DETAILS OF HER LIFE WERE EXPOSED
TO THE PUBLIC, MUCH ABOUT MONROE REMAINS
SHROUDED IN MYSTERY.

woman, between fact and fabrication, perhaps
it does not matter. The tangle of the truth,
Monroe's exaggerations of her past, and false
stories spread by her publicists contribute layers
of mystery and interest to the story of the woman
who became a US icon.

2

THE EARLY LIFE OF NORMA JEAN

Marilyn Monroe was born Norma Jean Mortenson on June 1, 1926, in Los Angeles, California. Norma Jean's mother was Gladys Baker, who had entered her first marriage when she was in her teens. Her second marriage ended just before Norma Jean was born, when Gladys was in her mid-twenties. Norma Jean was Gladys's third child. During her marriage to her second husband, Edward Mortenson, Gladys was also regularly seeing a man named Charles Stanley Gifford. This fact has made it impossible to

▸ NORMA JEAN IN 1928

identify Norma Jean's father with certainty. Most biographers agree that either Mortenson or Gifford must have been her father. Although Norma Jean took Mortenson's surname legally, neither man accepted the role of father in Norma Jean's life. Norma Jean was later baptized and would be raised as Norma Jean Baker.

Though Gladys loved her daughter, she immediately had a hard time filling the role of mother. She worked in the film industry and enjoyed her job, income, and active social life. Not wanting to add in the task of raising a daughter, Gladys placed Norma Jean in the care of foster parents just 12 days after her birth.

THE BOLENDERS

Gladys's mother, Della Mae Monroe, recommended Gladys seek out Ida and Wayne Bolender as foster parents. They were a strict but loving couple who cared for a number of foster children over the years in their Hawthorne, California, home.

Naming Norma

A few different stories exist about how Norma Jean got her name. One popular story is that her mother named her after screen actress Norma Talmadge. Many have romanticized this story by adding that Jean Harlow—Norma Jean's predecessor, a sexy, platinum-blonde star—was the inspiration for her middle name. However, Harlow did not get her

Norma Jean lived in relative happiness and comfort with the Bolenders for the first seven years of her life. During this time, Gladys visited her daughter on Sundays, often accompanied by her best friend, coworker Grace McKee. Some of Gladys and Grace's favorite things to do with Norma Jean were taking her to the movies or going to see the homes of movie stars living in the area. With these influences, along with living near Hollywood, the glamour and intrigue conveyed by celebrity life often surrounded Norma Jean while she was growing up.

Shortly after Norma Jean turned seven, Gladys decided she wanted to reclaim her daughter. But Ida had grown to love Norma Jean as her own, and some accounts claim she wanted to adopt her. However, Gladys was determined to get her daughter back. An unexpected tragedy served as the perfect opportunity for the transition.

In June 1933, Norma Jean's best friend was a dog named Tippy. He was a stray the Bolenders had agreed to let her keep. He was also a nuisance to the neighbors. According to most versions of the story, one neighbor got so fed up with Tippy's constant barking that he killed the dog. Norma Jean was so traumatized by the death of her beloved pet that Ida felt Gladys should step in.

▲ GLADYS CONTINUED TO APPEAR AND THEN ABANDON
NORMA JEAN THROUGHOUT HER LIFE.

GLADYS

Gladys and Grace came to comfort Norma Jean.
They helped her bury Tippy and pack up her
things. Then they whisked her off to Hollywood.
In August 1933, Gladys had saved enough money
to buy a house, where she hoped Norma Jean
would spend the rest of her childhood. But that
was not to be.

Gladys became overwhelmed by the
responsibility of paying for her new home and
raising her daughter on her own in the midst
of the worldwide economic slump known as
the Great Depression. She was not sleeping
or eating well, and her stress gradually turned

into depression. Renting part of her home to another family, the Atkinsons, helped for a little while. But in October, Gladys received two pieces of devastating news. The first was that her son from her first marriage, who had been in his early teens, had died of kidney trouble in August. The second was that Gladys's grandfather had committed suicide, likely due to financial difficulties. Already deeply troubled, Gladys became a complete wreck. Grace was concerned about her friend and decided to get her medical help. Unfortunately, that help came in the form of medications with side effects that were poorly understood. The medicines only worsened Gladys's condition.

By early 1934, Gladys was sent to a rest home, and when she did not improve, she was hospitalized indefinitely for psychiatric care. Norma Jean was left in the care of Grace and the Atkinsons for the rest of that year, not clearly understanding why or where her mother had gone.

GRACE

Grace loved her best friend's little girl, and, at this point, she wanted to give Norma Jean a more normal childhood. She even thought Norma Jean could become a star someday. Grace applied to become Norma Jean's legal guardian. But Norma Jean would not be able to live with Grace until after the state had investigated and approved her as a fit guardian. This meant Norma Jean was shuffled around again, first to Grace's Los Angeles neighbors and then to Grace's aunt, Ana Lower, whom Norma Jean called Aunt Ana. Aunt Ana would make Norma Jean feel more loved and accepted than anyone else had in her life.

Around this time, Grace fell in love with a man named Doc Goddard. In August 1935, Grace and Doc were married. Doc had three children from a previous marriage, and Grace had become Norma Jean's legal guardian. For a few weeks, Norma Jean and the Goddards lived together as a family. Then something changed. Perhaps the Goddards were in a tough financial situation with so many children to care for or the sudden mixing of families caused strain on their marriage. Whatever the reason, on September 13, Grace placed nine-year-old Norma Jean in the Los Angeles Orphans' Home.

THE ORPHANS' HOME
"The world around me just crumbled," Norma Jean later remembered of the time she spent at the Orphans' Home. "It seemed nobody wanted me."[1] Norma Jean got less attention at the

Orphans' Home, and she was often teased at school.

Grace visited Norma Jean often, assuring her she was loved and telling her if she wanted to, she could become a star someday. According to most accounts, Norma Jean lived at the Orphans' Home for nearly two years, though it may have been as little as nine months.

Sometime between 1936 and 1937, Grace decided to take Norma Jean home from the orphanage for good. But yet again, Norma Jean's chance at having a family was shattered. Some say Norma Jean caused so much strain in the Goddards' home that Grace and Doc decided she would be better off somewhere else. Others claim Grace sent her away after Doc molested her. Whatever the case, Norma Jean was placed in the care of her beloved Aunt Ana in 1938.

Tall Tales

Later in her life, Norma Jean would give many accounts of the years she spent in foster care and at the Orphans' Home. Though they may not have been the happiest times, most of her stories were grossly exaggerated. And some stories were stolen from the lives of other children Norma Jean met while she was growing up. One of the people whose lives gave her the most useful story material was Beebe Goddard, one of Doc's daughters. Like Norma Jean, Beebe had been in foster care for a while, and she had had a nightmarish experience there. Beebe had been molested, raped, neglected, and forced to do hard labor in foster care. As Norma Jean was becoming a star, she realized she could gain more sympathy from the public if she passed off Beebe's horrifying experiences as her own.

Half Sister Miracle

In 1938, 12-year-old Norma Jean learned she had a half sister. Her name was Berniece Baker Miracle. She was 19 years old, recently married, and pregnant with her first child. Norma Jean was thrilled. A family member said, "[Norma Jean] wanted to know Berniece, everything about her. She wrote her a letter and sent a picture of herself. Berniece wrote back immediately with her own photograph. It was an amazing connection from the start. From the very beginning, Norma Jean signed all of her letters 'Your Sister.'"[3] The sisters visited each other from time to time and remained lifelong friends.

AUNT ANA

The years she spent with Aunt Ana seemed to help heal some of Norma Jean's emotional wounds. Norma Jean later recalled of Aunt Ana, "She changed my whole life. She was the only person who loved me and understood me. . . . She was all kindness and love."[2] Norma Jean especially appreciated Aunt Ana's support of her dream to become an actress. Aunt Ana continued to be an important fixture in Norma Jean's life throughout the 1940s. However, she was in her sixties and beginning to have health problems. She felt she could no longer properly care for Norma Jean, who was quickly growing into a young woman.

JIM DOUGHERTY

Around 1940, Norma Jean moved back in with the Goddards. Life was good for a while. She bonded with Beebe, one of Doc's daughters. She was happy at her new school, Van Nuys High

▲ NORMA JEAN, *FAR LEFT*, WITH ANA LOWER, *SECOND FROM LEFT*, WHOM SHE FONDLY CALLED AUNT ANA

School, where she made a lot of friends. Best of all, one of the Goddards' neighbors had a handsome 19-year-old son, Jim Dougherty, to whom Norma Jean took a liking. Though Jim could not help but take notice of Norma Jean, he felt he was too old for her.

In December 1941, the Goddards and the Doughertys arranged for Jim to take Norma Jean as his date to a Christmas party. Whatever romantic feelings the two had for each other came into full bloom that evening. It was obvious to Grace that Jim and Norma Jean had fallen for each other, and she encouraged their budding romance.

In 1942, Doc was offered a job on the East Coast and planned to relocate the family. But whether his company would relocate only blood relatives or Doc could not find it in his heart to love or support another child, Norma Jean would not be going with them. Not wanting to return Norma Jean to the Orphans' Home for the last few years of her adolescence, Grace came up with a plan. Norma Jean would turn 16 that summer, the legal marrying age in the state of California. If Jim agreed to marry her, Norma Jean would have a home and a family. She would be loved and cared for, and she would never have to feel like an orphan again.

Eager to keep Norma Jean from any further suffering, Jim married her on June 19, 1942, just weeks after her sixteenth birthday. The Goddards had already moved away, and Gladys was not able to attend the wedding. Despite these slights, Norma Jean was excited to be Jim's wife. It is uncertain whether she hoped for happily ever after with Jim, but it is safe to say she never expected her marriage to set her on the path toward superstardom.

———— •◆• ————

▲ NORMA JEAN ON JUNE 19, 1942, THE DAY SHE MARRIED JIM DOUGHERTY

3

AN AMBITIOUS BEAUTY

s Jim and Norma Jean settled into married life in California, World War II (1939–1945) was raging abroad. Norma Jean dropped out of school—a move she would come to regret—to focus on being a wife. Jim wanted to serve his country by joining the military. This idea made Norma Jean feel betrayed. Her chaotic childhood had left her with deep insecurities, and she felt if Jim went away to war, he would be abandoning her. Jim understood and sought a compromise. In 1943, he joined the US Merchant Marine.

▶ JIM AND NORMA JEAN ON CATALINA ISLAND, CALIFORNIA, IN 1943

He was stationed on Catalina Island, California, just off the coast of Los Angeles. Though he would sometimes be at sea for months, Norma Jean could live with him there.

THE RIVETING WORKER

Jim took an overseas assignment in 1944. Norma Jean took a job at Radio Plane, a factory in Burbank, California, applying varnish to cloth that was used to manufacture planes. It was there her beauty caught a photographer's eye for the first time. David Conover was part of a group of US Army photographers who came to the Radio Plane factory to photograph pretty girls contributing to the war effort. The photographers could take additional photos of the girls to sell to magazines if they liked. Of all the young women at the factory, Conover enjoyed working with Norma Jean the most. He recognized her natural talent for modeling. Conover later noted,

The Merchant Marine

The Merchant Marine that Jim joined is a nation's fleet of commercial ships, which transport either cargo or passengers. The Merchant Marine was vital in World War II, carrying supplies, weapons, and soldiers where needed. Due to their important role, merchant ships were often targeted, and though not fighting as soldiers, the men who operated them were often killed. Despite their courageous service in the war, those who served in the US Merchant Marine

"There was a luminous quality in her face—a fragility combined with something astonishingly vibrant."[1]

Others were equally impressed with Norma Jean's photographs and with how easy she was to work with. She took direction well. She asked a lot of questions and was constantly trying to become a better model. Norma Jean's hard work soon paid off. In August 1945, Emmeline Snively signed the 19-year-old brunette to her renowned Blue Book Modeling Agency in Los Angeles.

Through the modeling agency, Norma Jean got further training and was soon in high demand. Her smiling image began appearing on many magazine covers. Norma Jean's work ethic proved to be as important as her looks to her success as a model. Snively said, "She was the hardest worker I ever handled. She wanted to learn, wanted to be somebody, more than anybody I ever met before in my life."[2] After only a year with the Blue Book Modeling

"I just knew I could make it. I would take home photographs of myself to study how I looked and if I could improve myself posing in front of a mirror for hours. The next day I would see the photographer . . . and ask, 'What did I do wrong in this photo?' or 'Why didn't this photo come out better?' When they told me, I would never make that mistake again. I believed in myself. I just had to make it. I was determined to make it. Nothing was going to get in my way."[3]

—Marilyn Monroe

▲ PHOTOGRAPHERS TOOK NOTICE OF NORMA JEAN'S BEAUTY AND WERE IMPRESSED WITH HER EFFORTS TO CREATE QUALITY PHOTOGRAPHS.

Agency, Norma Jean had appeared on more than 30 magazine covers.

DREAMING BIGGER

Norma Jean was proud of her growing portfolio and eager to see if her talent for modeling would come across in film. But first, Snively said Norma Jean would have to go blonde. There was a growing demand for blonde models, and Snively did not think Norma Jean could make it as a brunette. Norma Jean was skeptical but agreed to dye her hair. Afterward, she said, "I saw it worked. Miss Snively sure knew what she was telling me. I began to get more modeling assignments."[4] Some of these assignments were with famous photographer Andre de Dienes, who took several iconic photographs of Norma Jean in the late 1940s and early 1950s.

While Norma Jean was thrilled with her success and determined to make her way to the big screen, Jim preferred she play the role of dutiful housewife. But Norma Jean had no intention of putting her husband's dreams ahead of her own and continued modeling. Adding to the tension between Jim and Norma Jean, Gladys was released from treatment in 1946 and came to live with them. Norma Jean shared the only bed with her mother and crowded her husband out of her home—and her heart. In the spring of 1946, Norma Jean filed for divorce. Shortly after, Norma Jean's relationship with her mother also reached a breaking point, and Gladys returned to treatment. That summer, Norma Jean was free to pursue her dream of becoming a movie star.

A TICKET TO HOLLYWOOD

Snively kept her eye out for potential film opportunities for Norma Jean. An opportunity came knocking in 1946 after Howard Hughes—

a famous businessman, aviator, and filmmaker—saw Norma Jean's image on a magazine cover. He was impressed and made arrangements for Norma Jean to have a screen test at his studio, Radio-Keith-Orpheum (RKO) Pictures. However, the fact that Norma Jean had captured Hughes's interest also made her attractive to other studios, including Twentieth Century Fox.

That summer, Norma Jean met with Ben Lyon, the talent scout and casting director at Fox. He had her read a few lines of a script and liked her enough to have her come back for a screen test. Norma Jean was not given any lines for this trial screen test. She later described her experience to a friend:

> *I walked across the set; I had to light a cigarette, inhale, then blow the smoke out, get up, then go upstage, cross, look out a window, sit down, come downstage, and then exit the set.*[5]

Even without any lines spoken, Norma Jean's presence on film was magic. One of the men who reviewed her screen test said, "I got a cold chill. This girl had something I hadn't seen since silent pictures. She had a kind of fantastic beauty."[6]

Darryl Zanuck, the head of Fox, was not so impressed. He preferred brunette actresses to blonde ones, and Norma Jean had no acting

▲ WITH HER NEWLY BLONDE HAIR AND NAME CHANGED
TO MARILYN MONROE, NORMA JEAN WAS READY TO TAKE
ON HOLLYWOOD.

experience whatsoever. Still, everyone else was
so excited about her that Zanuck signed her to a
six-month contract. In August 1946, it became
official: Norma Jean was a Twentieth Century
Fox starlet. There was just one thing left to do
before the transformation from model to actress
was complete.

Lyon explained that Norma Jean Dougherty
was not a name for a star and was hard to
pronounce. After much discussion, Norma Jean
and Lyon agreed to couple Gladys's maiden name,
Monroe, with the first name of an actress Lyon
had loved: Marilyn Miller. And that was the
beginning of Marilyn Monroe.

4

THE MAKING OF MARILYN MONROE

t Fox, Monroe was one of many stars in training. She and other pretty, young starlets received lessons in acting, singing, dancing, and other skills to prepare them for a career in film. All had signed contracts that allowed the studio to fire them after six months if they were not considered star material.

Monroe did not get any roles during her first six months at Fox. However, still willing to give her a chance, Fox renewed her contract in February 1947. During this time, Monroe got a

▶ MONROE, *MIDDLE*, PRACTICED DANCING, SINGING, AND ACTING TO BECOME A STAR.

After being dropped by Fox, Monroe attached herself to talent agent Lucille Carroll and Lucille's husband, both of whom had connections in Hollywood. Monroe lived with the couple for a while, but the Carrolls were unprepared for her neediness. In her insecurity, Monroe all but took over their lives. Lucille later said of that period, "[Monroe] didn't know how to handle her life . . . she fell apart. We liked her, but we needed her and her craziness out of our lives."[1]

chance to try out her acting skills in a series of tiny parts that had no chance of getting her noticed, but were at least a start. While there is some confusion about which role Monroe officially filmed first, her first films were *Dangerous Years,* released in 1947, and *Scudda Hoo! Scudda Hay!,* released in 1948. But these small roles were not enough to convince Fox Monroe had what it took to be a successful actress. The studio dropped her after her first year.

COLUMBIA PICTURES

Monroe was crushed, but she was far from ready to give up on her dream. She spent the next few months trying to attract the attention of other big names in the film industry. In early 1948, Monroe's search for a second chance led her to Joe Schenck. He was running Fox along with Zanuck. He was also notorious for his extravagant parties, which Harry Cohn, head of Columbia Pictures studio, often attended. Schenck and Monroe gradually developed a friendship. As

Zanuck was not ready to take Monroe back at Fox, Schenck called in a favor from Cohn and got her a screen test at Columbia. Though unimpressed by her, Cohn ultimately signed Monroe for six months beginning on March 9, 1948.

At Columbia, Monroe's instructors became important figures in her life. She began a brief romantic relationship with voice coach Fred Karger, who was training her for a minor role in the musical *Ladies of the Chorus.* Her acting coach at Columbia, Natasha Lytess, became the instructor she most wished to please. However, *Ladies of the Chorus* was not a success, and Columbia sent Monroe on her way after her first six months.

JOHNNY HYDE

Monroe rang in the new year of 1949 at a party that drew many influential people in Hollywood. One was talent agent Johnny Hyde, who fell deeply in love with Monroe almost immediately after they met. A short, middle-aged man in poor health, Hyde may not have been physically attractive to Monroe. But she recognized his ability to help her become a star, so she responded to his advances.

In early 1949, shortly after she met Hyde, Monroe auditioned for a role in a Marx Brothers film called *Love Happy*. The Marx Brothers were a family of five brothers who had much success making comedic films in the 1930s and 1940s and appeared in various film and television cameos in the 1950s and 1960s. The story goes that Groucho Marx asked if Monroe could walk, explaining, "This role calls for a young lady who can walk by me in such a manner as to . . . cause smoke to issue from my ears."[2] Monroe strode across the room, swinging her hips seductively, and got the part. Her role in *Love Happy* lasted only 38 seconds, but those few seconds helped establish her as the sex symbol she soon became.

GOLDEN DREAMS

Despite the attention she got for her appearance in *Love Happy*, Monroe failed to pick up a contract with another major studio. She had

The Picture That Discovered
MARILYN MONROE

L♥VE
HAPPY

ILONA MASSEY · VERA-ELLEN
MARION HUTTON

starring
THE Marx Bros.

▲ MONROE'S ROLE IN LOVE HAPPY WAS BRIEF, BUT IT GOT
HER NOTICED.

frequently been late to the set, wasting her coworkers' time and the studio's money. Being out of steady work for so long, Monroe claims she became desperate for money around this time. She was willing to do something drastic.

Tom Kelley was a photographer who had worked with Monroe in the past and had been kind to her. When he asked her to pose nude for a calendar image in May 1949, she reluctantly agreed. Monroe knew if she ever did become a star and was recognized in the nude photos, she would suffer public humiliation and could lose everything. When asked years later why Monroe had posed for him, Kelley said, "I think it was partially a favor . . . and she really did need the money."[4] Monroe knew the chances of her being recognized were slim. But just to be sure, she signed her model release for the two calendar images as Mona Monroe. Her secret seemed safe for the time being.

ON THE RISE

During the summer of 1949, Monroe's career was not progressing as she had hoped. Hyde helped her get a small part in *A Ticket to Tomahawk*, a movie produced by Fox, but the film was a flop. Monroe's personal life also was not going well. Hyde, having left his wife and children for Monroe by this time, was pressuring her to marry him. Hyde loved Monroe and believed she could become a star. But he was also verbally abusive toward Monroe, and she did not love him back.

At the end of 1949, Hyde finally began to make good on his promise to launch Monroe to stardom. He and Lucille Carroll, head of the talent department at Metro-Goldwyn-Mayer (MGM), teamed up to convince respected director John Huston to let Monroe audition for his film *The Asphalt Jungle*. Monroe was cast in the role of Angela, the young mistress of a criminal older man. It was not a starring role, but it would require more work than any of her previous parts. Monroe looked to Lytess, her acting coach from Columbia, rather than Huston, to help her through it. This caused some strain on the set, but Huston let Lytess stay. The film was well received, earning four Oscar nominations and bringing Monroe closer to stardom.

In 1950, Monroe took a couple mediocre roles before Hyde came through for her again. That spring, he got her a part in the new Fox film *All About Eve*. Monroe played Miss Caswell, an aspiring actress. And she was brilliant. *All About Eve* was a huge success. The film earned 14 Oscar nominations, a record that was tied by the 1997 film *Titanic* but remained unbeaten as of 2012.

THE BEGINNING

However, in December 1950, shortly after *All*

Reading on Set

Monroe was constantly reading to educate herself. On the set of *All About Eve*, writer and director Joe Mankiewicz was surprised to find her reading *Letters to a Young Poet* by Rainer Maria Rilke. When he asked her about the book, Monroe responded,

You see, in my whole life I haven't read hardly anything at all. . . . So what I do is, every now and then I go into the Pickwick [book shop] and just look around. I leaf through some books, and when I read something that interests me—I buy the book. So last night I bought this one.[5]

She felt embarrassed by this, but Mankiewicz assured her that was the best way to go about it. She thanked

About Eve was released, Hyde died of a heart attack, and Monroe sunk into a depression. Although Monroe did not have romantic feelings for Hyde, she did end up loving him, as he had done more for her than most other people in her life. His death was a heartbreaking loss for her. A few days after his funeral, Lytess experienced what was perhaps the start of Monroe's self-destructive behavior.

Monroe was living with Lytess, who returned home early to find Monroe lying limp in her bedroom. Her mouth was full of Nembutal sleeping pills, but thankfully she had not yet swallowed them. At the time, Lytess was terrified. Later, it seemed odd that Monroe had not thought to wash the pills down with something if she truly wished to die. More likely, it was a way for Monroe to attract the attention she craved.

Fortunately, Monroe had a lot to live for over the next several years. Before he died, Hyde made some arrangements to help Monroe take advantage of her successes in *The Asphalt Jungle* and *All About Eve*. Negotiations he began with Fox to sign Monroe to a long-term contract came to fruition in the spring of 1951. Monroe was on the edge of stardom.

———•◆•———

▲ MONROE LIVED WITH ACTING COACH AND FRIEND
NATASHA LYTESS OFF AND ON IN THE EARLY 1950S.

THE BRIGHTEST STAR

In the early 1950s, Monroe played supporting roles in several films. She was nearly always cast as a blonde bombshell who relied more on her body than her brain. In 1951, she played four of these roles in *Home Town Story*, *As Young as You Feel*, *Love Nest*, and *Let's Make It Legal*. By this time, she had also met many of the people who would feature prominently in the rest of her life. These people included columnist Sid Skolsky and playwright Arthur Miller. Monroe and Miller met on the set of *As Young as You Feel* and

▶ IN 1951, MONROE WAS MAKING MANY FILMS AND QUICKLY BECOMING A STAR.

would not see each other again for approximately four years. But during those years, she fondly remembered Miller as one of the only people who took her seriously as an actress.

Monroe met her friend Skolsky at famous Hollywood hangout Schwab's drugstore. In the fall of 1951, he helped her get a role in the film *Clash by Night*. Skolsky knew the producer had family connections that would ensure huge publicity for the film and the actors lucky enough to be cast in it. Fox agreed to loan its rising star to RKO to do the film, but as it turned out, Monroe's career may not have needed the boost.

THE CALENDAR GIRL MEETS A BASEBALL STAR

In early 1952, after acting in another fluffy film called *We're Not Married*, Monroe landed her first major dramatic role. She played Nell, a woman who was mentally ill, in *Don't Bother to Knock*. Also around this time, Monroe met the man who would have perhaps the most impact on her life: recently retired baseball legend Joe DiMaggio.

The story goes that DiMaggio saw some publicity photos Monroe had taken with another baseball player. He thought this meant the voluptuous star was also a baseball fan, and he could not resist the combination. He wanted to

▲ JOE DiMAGGIO BECAME A PROMINENT FIGURE IN
MONROE'S LIFE.

meet Monroe, so a friend helped him arrange
a date. As usual, Monroe was late, but she was
also dazzling. DiMaggio was quiet, even boring,
but Monroe was fascinated by the way he
commanded attention.

Just weeks after Monroe's date with
DiMaggio, the unthinkable happened. Someone
had recognized Monroe from the nude calendar
pictures Kelley had shot, and it was all over the
news. Fox executives were outraged, fearing the
public's reaction to the scandal. Monroe was
terrified it would be the end of her career. Not
knowing how to handle the situation, she sought
the advice of her Hollywood-savvy friend Skolsky.

Skolsky encouraged Monroe to go forward with a previously arranged interview for media outlet United Press International. After the interview was over, Monroe was to take the interviewer aside and confess she had posed for the pictures when she was desperate for money. She would say she did not want to lie about it and did not think she had done anything wrong. As Skolsky and Monroe had planned, the interviewer published the star's vulnerable confession. The public was fascinated with the story, and people were quick to forgive their star. Monroe rehearsed witty responses to questions she knew she would be asked, such as "What did you have on?" to which she coyly replied, "The radio."[1] Everyone was delighted with her sense of humor and the way she seemed seductive and innocent all at once.

Appendicitis

While filming *Monkey Business*, Monroe was suffering from appendicitis. Not wanting to delay filming, she settled for antibiotic treatment until the movie was finished. Afterward, she had her appendix removed. The scar is visible in later photos of her.

During this time, DiMaggio and Monroe's relationship developed into a highly publicized romance. He frequently visited her on the set of *Monkey Business*, which she was filming in March 1952. Since Monroe's more serious performance in

Don't Bother to Knock had been harshly criticized, *Monkey Business* found her back in her familiar role as a sexy secretary. It was Monroe's last minor role.

THE PLATINUM YEARS

In the summer of 1952, Monroe was cast in *Niagara*. Though Monroe came across beautifully on film, the movie was not very good. Monroe also behaved oddly on set. In addition to her usual lateness and dependence on acting coach Lytess, Monroe dressed more revealingly than her scenes called for. Tension had developed between Monroe and DiMaggio, likely adding to the insecurities that led Monroe to attract attention in this way. Just as Monroe had experienced in her marriage to Dougherty, DiMaggio wanted her to give up her career and settle down with him.

Instead, Monroe went on to star in one of her most successful and challenging films, the musical *Gentlemen Prefer Blondes*. Filming began late in 1952, and Monroe gave it her all. She had to sing, dance, and hold her own next to brunette beauty Jane Russell, another popular, voluptuous star. And Monroe did hold her own, especially during her memorable version of the song "Diamonds Are a Girl's Best Friend" in the film. She also got to show off her flair for comedic acting, which would benefit her throughout the rest of her career. The film was wildly successful, grossing more than $12 million (approximately $100 million today).

FAME AND MISFORTUNE

In March 1953, just days after she finished filming *Gentlemen Prefer Blondes*, Monroe began work on *How to Marry a Millionaire*. Monroe was exhausted from the back-to-back filming, and she was also worried about her mother, who had recently tried contacting her. With long hours working on set followed by long hours working with her acting coach, Monroe barely had time to sleep. She began relying on sleeping pills to help her take advantage of the few short hours she had to rest each day. Even so, her body could not keep up with her busy schedule, and Monroe was hospitalized after coming down with a virus. Her *How to Marry a Millionaire* costars appeared understanding of Monroe's health problems. However, other annoyances arose. Costar Lauren Bacall later complained it often took 15 or more takes for Monroe and Lytess to be satisfied with a scene.

▲ Monroe in *Gentlemen Prefer Blondes*

Monroe's hard work resulted in increasing fame in 1953. Her roles in *Gentlemen Prefer Blondes* and *How to Marry a Millionaire* showed she was not only beautiful but a talented comedian as well. Yet, Monroe wanted a chance to show she could handle more serious roles than the ones that had made her famous.

Monroe would tolerate one more frivolous role Fox chose for her before taking a stand. In *River of No Return*, Monroe was beautiful, and she sang and acted well. However, the summer of 1953, when the movie was made, was trying. Monroe was quickly becoming more dependent on the drugs she took to help her sleep. She also did not get along with the director of the film, Otto Preminger. Preminger did not respect Monroe, and he forced her to film dangerous scenes in a raging river. Monroe even twisted her ankle during filming. DiMaggio was with her on location. Though he clearly disapproved of Monroe's movie star lifestyle, he was protective of her, and his presence must have been a comfort. At the end of 1953, Fox told Monroe she would soon begin filming *The Girl in Pink Tights*—another role as a bouncy blonde in a fluffy musical. With

Grace and Gladys's Roles

Shortly before starting *River of No Return,* Monroe found out her some-times-guardian Grace had cancer. Though she tried her best to care for the dying woman, Monroe had her own demons to deal with. Grace was concerned about Monroe's use of prescription drugs. Grace's death in the fall of 1953 was a profound loss for Monroe, and her emotional pain likely fueled her increasing drug addiction.

Grace's illness also meant Monroe had to take over responsibility for her mother's care, which Grace had been overseeing. Monroe was constantly torn between her love for her mother and her resentment for being abandoned as a child. In addition, Gladys's mental illness made it difficult for Monroe to rebuild their relationship. On Monroe's twenty-seventh birthday, her mother allegedly claimed, "I don't remember giving birth to you."[2] Even when Gladys did acknowledge Monroe as her daughter, she was not supportive of the star's career. Despite their strained relationship, Monroe did all she could to help her mother and

▲ MONROE ON THE SET OF *RIVER OF NO RETURN*, WHERE
SHE TWISTED HER ANKLE DURING FILMING

this announcement, Monroe decided she had
tolerated enough professional abuse.

———◆———

6

IN AND OUT
OF CONTROL

anuary 1954 was an eventful
month for Monroe. She refused
to have anything to do with *The
Girl in Pink Tights*, spurring an
all-out war with Fox. The studio threatened to
suspend her contract, but she was not about
to back down. Besides, she had something far
more pleasant to focus on: DiMaggio had asked
Monroe to marry him.

Monroe wed DiMaggio on January 14,
1954, in San Francisco, California. Fans of the
two celebrities were thrilled, as was the press.

▶ MONROE AND DIMAGGIO ON THEIR WEDDING DAY,
JANUARY 14, 1954

Hundreds stood outside the city hall that day to catch a glimpse of the famous couple. Sensing Monroe was slipping out of their grasp, Fox executives lifted her suspension. They offered to let her read the script for *The Girl in Pink Tights* as a last-ditch effort to get her to do the film. DiMaggio and Monroe returned from their honeymoon in late January. Instead of going back to work for Fox, however, Monroe announced she would be leaving again on a trip to Japan with her new husband. The couple left for Japan on January 29.

MR. MONROE

The trip to Japan was really a business trip—and an ego trip—for DiMaggio. Baseball was huge in Japan, and he anticipated being mobbed by fans. It would be a welcome change, as Monroe often outshone him back home. When the couple arrived in Tokyo, Japan, the swarms of fans were there, but they all belonged to Monroe. As it became clear the people of Japan were far more fascinated with his wife than they were with him, DiMaggio grew angry.

Shortly after arriving in Japan, Monroe was invited to take a side trip to entertain US troops in Korea. DiMaggio wanted her to stay in Japan, but Monroe was determined to go.

▲ PERFORMING FOR TROOPS IN KOREA WAS A
WONDERFUL EXPERIENCE FOR MONROE, WHO DID SO
DESPITE HER NEW HUSBAND'S WISHES.

The tour lasted from February 16 to 19. Despite
the freezing February weather, Monroe wore
a curve-hugging, skin-baring gown when she
appeared in front of the thousands of soldiers.

The suggestive lyrics of the songs she sang were nearly drowned out at times by the soldiers' appreciative cheers. Such a warm reception made the performance one of Monroe's favorite memories.

Several days later, Monroe returned to Japan and a disgruntled DiMaggio. Some say DiMaggio, jealous of his wife's fame, beat her during their time in Japan. Certainly, the two fought during the trip, but they stayed together, continuing the rocky relationship.

Studying Singer Fitzgerald

Monroe often studied famous jazz singer Ella Fitzgerald's recordings to help improve her own singing. When Monroe found out a famous club in Hollywood had refused to let Fitzgerald perform because she was African American, Monroe was furious. She called up the club and let the management know Fitzgerald would be performing there and that Monroe would be in the audience every night Fitzgerald performed. In the end, Fitzgerald was allowed to perform, and the publicity Monroe's presence attracted was likely appreciated.

BACK TO WORK

In March, Fox finally gave up trying to force Monroe to act in *The Girl in Pink Tights*. To win back the star, Fox offered her roles that would showcase her singing, dancing, and comedic talents in *There's No Business Like Show Business* and *The Seven Year Itch*. Studio executives also promised her a new contract and a hefty bonus later in the year. Monroe accepted the deal and went to work on *There's No Business*

Like Show Business. Unfortunately, the problems that had always plagued her on set were getting worse. She was continually late, sometimes keeping the rest of the cast and crew waiting for up to six hours. Her abuse of prescription drugs was spiraling out of control, and she had such a hard time concentrating that it took her up to 50 takes to get even the simplest scenes right. In addition, Monroe's role in the film was overtly sexual, with skimpy outfits and lewd gestures and innuendos. DiMaggio was furious when he visited the set during a rehearsal of Monroe's steamiest number, "Heat Wave." Those close to the couple reported that DiMaggio was physically abusing Monroe at the time. Reviews of the film were mixed. The music was a hit, but many disliked Monroe's performance. A critic from the *New York Times* said her performance was "embarrassing to behold."[1]

THE SEVEN YEAR ITCH

Next up in the summer of 1954 was what many consider to be Monroe's greatest film, *The Seven Year Itch.* She was perfect for the role of the Girl, a naïvely sexy young woman who rents an apartment in the same building as a married man whose wife and children are away. The man is tempted to stray from his wife, but

▲ THE SCENE OF MONROE'S SKIRT BILLOWING OVER A SUBWAY GRATE BECAME FOREVER LINKED WITH HER IMAGE.

nothing much happens except a series of hilarious encounters and over-the-top fantasies. As always, Monroe brought her baggage of habitual lateness, insecurity, and a jealous husband to the set. Though these problems cost Monroe's coworkers their time, money, and patience, the profit she brought the studio made the extra effort worth it.

An image from this movie became one of Monroe's most iconic. In the scene, she stands over a subway grate with her white dress billowing around her as she tries to hold it down. It was filmed in New York in the wee hours of a chilly September morning. Fans turned out by the thousands. Photographers clamored to capture tantalizing publicity images. The footage shot ended up being far too risqué for the 1950s and was toned down in the film. Monroe's skirt billowed a bit too high, giving the crowd a glimpse of her panties from time to time.

DiMaggio was part of that crowd, and he was not happy. When the couple returned to their hotel after the scene was shot, there was a loud fight. DiMaggio hit Monroe hard enough to leave bruises that had to be disguised with makeup for the next day's filming. She later told her hairdresser, "Joe beat me up twice. The first time,

"He was smacking her around, yes. He didn't seem too ashamed of it, either. He said that she brought the worst out in him, that he wasn't usually that kind of man. He said she was spoiled and very self-centered and it drove him crazy."[2]
—One of DiMaggio's friends on his relationship with Monroe

I warned him. 'Don't ever do that again.' I'm not going to stand for it."[3] And she did not. In October, Monroe filed for divorce.

A few months later, another war began between Monroe and Fox. Fox was determined to hold her to her contract and wanted her to play another role she felt was demeaning. When she refused, Fox used the press to punish her, painting her as a high-maintenance diva who could not act. Monroe had had enough of Hollywood. She wanted a fresh start and more control over her career. She decided the best way to get it would be to leave Fox and start her own company. At the end of 1954, Monroe moved to New York and established Marilyn Monroe

Wrong Door Raid

Monroe may have thought abusive ex-husband DiMaggio was out of her life when she divorced him, but DiMaggio became obsessed with her. He even hired a private investigator to spy on her. This resulted in an embarrassing break-in at an apartment where DiMaggio suspected Monroe was spending time with a lover. What was believed to be Monroe's car was parked outside the apartment. DiMaggio brought friends along to help with the bust, including famous singer Frank Sinatra (whom, in an ironic twist, would later end up dating Monroe). Upon breaking down the door, the men found only one person in the apartment: the resident, woken from her sleep and terrified by the break-in. It turned out Monroe had been nearby in an apartment a few doors down visiting a friend. The men were sued

Productions (MMP) with partner, friend, and well-known photographer Milton Greene.

NEW YORK

Monroe lived in New York City for one year, working to improve her acting skills by studying under actor and instructor Lee Strasberg at the Actors Studio. Strasberg's wife, Paula, a former stage actress, was also a constant presence. Around the same time, Greene arranged for Monroe to start seeing a psychoanalyst. The therapy was supposed to help Monroe improve herself both professionally and personally, but it also brought up painful memories of her past. Monroe dealt with the pain and exhaustion she felt during her year in New York by taking more sleeping pills and stimulants. As taking these types of pills was an accepted practice at the time, most of the people close to Monroe showed only mild concern at her behavior.

But things were about to get a little bit brighter. Monroe was making headway in negotiations with Fox, which had been struggling without its star. *The Seven Year Itch* was released and earned glowing reviews. Finally, in December 1955, Fox offered Monroe a generous new contract. Her pay would be significantly increased, and she would have a high degree of

▲ MONROE BEGAN SEEING A THERAPIST—AND BEGAN
TAKING MORE PILLS—DURING HER YEAR IN NEW YORK.

control over the films she made. And—though
she would be required to make four films with
Fox—she would also be free to make films with
other studios. Monroe accepted the terms and

moved back to Los Angeles, where she would soon begin work on *Bus Stop*.

Around this same time, Monroe also began a new romance. She began secretly dating Arthur Miller, who had been on her mind during her marriage to DiMaggio.

———•◆•———

Arthur Miller

Arthur Miller was a famous US playwright. He wrote *Death of a Salesman*, for which he received a Pulitzer Prize. *The Crucible* is another well-known play by Miller. He also wrote the script for what would be Monroe's last completed film, *The Misfits*. Miller's play *After the Fall*, written after Monroe's death, was widely believed to be based on his relationship with her.

Monroe began filming *Bus Stop* in early 1956. Parts of the movie were filmed on location in Arizona and Idaho, so Monroe was shuttled between the two. Due to health problems caused by bronchitis, her drug use, the exertion of traveling, or a combination of these factors, Monroe was often absent from the set. When she was on set, she was unfocused. However, her work with Strasberg and his wife Paula seemed to be paying off. The *Hollywood Reporter* praised her for bringing her character to life

▶ MONROE IN A SCENE FROM THE 1956 FILM *BUS STOP*

with "a sensitivity, a poignancy, and an apparent understanding that Miss Monroe did not display before."[1]

While Monroe filmed *Bus Stop*, Miller sought a divorce from his wife so he would be free to pursue a serious relationship with Monroe. But something else was standing in the couple's way. Miller was in trouble with the House Un-American Activities Committee (HUAC), which accused him of associating with Communists. The HUAC was an organization that investigated anyone suspected of being involved in Communist activities. Against

The HUAC

Established in 1938, the HUAC was a committee of the House of Representatives devoted to investigating Communist influence in the United States. In the late 1940s, Congress member (and future president) Richard Nixon played a key role in the organization. The committee was created during the Cold War, a rivalry between the United States and the Soviet Union that developed after the countries' alliance dissolved after World War II. The United States feared the power of Soviet Communists would spread. The HUAC targeted several celebrity figures it suspected were involved in Communist activities, including Arthur Miller. The HUAC's practices were highly controversial and viewed by many as violating people's rights to freedom and privacy. The HUAC's practices added to the hysteria concerning communism already present in the 1950s. By the 1960s, however, the organization's relevance began waning. The HUAC was renamed the

the advice of Fox executives, Monroe stood by Miller during the investigation. At the end of June, after Miller obtained his divorce and before Monroe flew to London to work on her next film, the two were married.

DISAPPOINTING PRINCES

Monroe's next project in 1956 was *The Prince and the Showgirl*, which was the first film produced by Monroe's company, MMP. Famous actor Laurence Olivier was her costar and director in the lavish period piece. As the first film she both starred in and produced, *The Prince and the Showgirl* should have been a major triumph for Monroe, but everything went wrong. Monroe and Olivier could barely stand each other. Monroe's abuse of prescription drugs was now often combined with alcohol, and it continued affecting her work. Olivier's performance was lackluster, the plot was boring, and the pace was too slow. After the disappointing film, Monroe returned to New York and moved in with her new husband.

Rumors had spread that Monroe and Miller's marriage

My Week with Marilyn

The 2011 film *My Week with Marilyn* is based on the memoirs of British assistant director Colin Clark during the filming of *The Prince and the Showgirl*. Now a documentary filmmaker, Clark claimed to have had a brief romance with Monroe while they worked on the film, not long after her marriage to Arthur Miller.

▲ ARTHUR MILLER AND MONROE WORKED TOGETHER FOR MUCH OF THEIR MARRIAGE, WHICH BECAME STRAINED SOON AFTER IT BEGAN.

was already troubled. Some suggest Miller was critical of Monroe's work on *The Prince and the Showgirl*. Many biographers relate the story of Monroe finding Miller's journal left open to a page where he had written about his wife's flaws. Also around this time, Monroe became pregnant but suffered a miscarriage. Perhaps due to these struggles, Monroe made no films in 1957 and claimed to enjoy the simplicity of life outside of Hollywood.

COMEDY OR TRAGEDY?

After her miscarriage, Monroe's depression deepened. With nothing else to distract her from her sorrow, she turned more and more to pills, champagne, and food. By the time she finally returned to work in the summer of 1958 to film *Some Like It Hot*, she had visibly gained weight. The weight gain was not the only thing clouding Monroe's work. Her addiction to drugs and alcohol was worse than ever and made her a horror to work with. She was prone to angry outbursts. She also kept a red thermos full of vermouth, a fortified wine, on set and drank from it after each take.

Monroe became pregnant again during filming, but she suffered a second miscarriage. Her drug abuse is believed to be the cause of that miscarriage. Despite Monroe's tumultuous professional and personal situations, *Some Like It Hot* was a hit. Monroe

Notes from the Cast and Crew

Some Like It Hot director Billy Wilder was understandably frustrated with Monroe's behavior during filming. He recalled, "There were days when I could have killed her, I admit it. I knew, of course, that she had serious problems."[2] Actor Tony Curtis, Monroe's love interest in the film, famously described the experience of kissing her as "like kissing Hitler."[3]

▲ ALTHOUGH MONROE'S PERFORMANCE IN *SOME LIKE IT HOT* WAS A GREAT SUCCESS, SHE EXPERIENCED MANY PERSONAL STRUGGLES DURING FILMING.

won a Golden Globe for Best Performance by an Actress in a Motion Picture–Comedy Or Musical for her role. She may have had some film magic left in her, but the loss of her second baby was difficult to overcome. Monroe would not appear in another film until 1960, two years before her death.

———•◆•———

onroe entered 1960 starring as French actor Yves Montand's love interest in *Let's Make Love*. The script was awful, so Miller was eventually hired to rewrite parts of it. Monroe was not excited to have her husband on set. She also supposedly lost respect for Miller for agreeing to do the rewrite instead of supporting the Writers Guild strike going on at the time.

Monroe's relationship with costar Montand added tension to her troubled marriage with Miller. Though Montand was fed up with

▸ MONROE AND *LET'S MAKE LOVE* COSTAR YVES MONTAND

Monroe's unpredictable behavior on set, he apparently sensed her vulnerability and her dwindling love for her husband. The two stars' on-screen romance spread into their off-screen lives. Their real affair made for electric love scenes in the film and, when it was discovered, great publicity for *Let's Make Love*.

THE FINAL FILM

In the summer of 1960, Monroe started work on what would be her last completed film, *The Misfits*. The film had an all-star cast and crew, including actor Clark Gable and director John Huston, who had worked with Monroe in *The Asphalt Jungle*. At this point, Monroe was abusing many different prescription drugs, and she was supplementing them with alcohol— usually champagne. Her marriage with Miller was virtually over, a situation made worse by the fact that he had written the script for *The Misfits*. Miller seemed to be using his position as the film's screenwriter to get back at his wife. He was constantly making changes to the script and forcing Monroe to relearn her lines. Many believe Miller partially based *The Misfits* script on his relationship with Monroe.

Around the time of filming, Monroe had sunk so deep into addiction that doctors began expressing concern. As a result, Monroe sought Dr. Ralph Greenson, who would continue prescribing her the dangerous drugs. Monroe came to rely on Greenson to fuel her addiction.

It was not long until exhaustion, the extreme heat of the Arizona filming location, and the combination of the drugs and alcohol became too much for Monroe. She was flown back to Los Angeles and admitted to the hospital, causing serious delays in filming.

The stress on the set of *The Misfits* affected everyone involved in the movie, but Gable seemed especially vulnerable. He

Dr. Ralph Greenson

Dr. Ralph Greenson was Monroe's psychoanalyst and trusted friend until her death. She consulted with him every day, and he eventually became like family. Monroe was able to express her deepest frustrations to him. In return, Greenson relieved her anguish with the drugs she craved. In fact, many believe he prescribed a combination of drugs that later proved fatal. Whether or not Greenson was responsible for Monroe's death, he did seem to stretch the boundaries of professionalism with his patient. Greenson began exerting control over Monroe's personal life. He hired a housekeeper, Eunice Murray, to keep an eye on her and report to him about her behavior. He also meddled in Monroe's career and love life. After Monroe's death, a Los Angeles County prosecutor revealed to the *Los Angeles Times* transcripts from what he claimed were secret tapes of Monroe talking about herself and her life that she had recorded for Greenson. The transcripts were shockingly candid and often vulgar, but there is no proof the tapes ever existed.

made an effort to look after his troubled costar. At one point, when Huston considered changing the script in a way that would be unflattering to Monroe, Gable even threatened to quit. When Gable died of a heart attack in November, just after *The Misfits* had been completed, Monroe blamed herself for causing him added stress.

COMMITMENT PROBLEMS

In January 1961, the weak thread keeping Monroe and Miller together finally snapped. Monroe obtained a quick divorce. However, instead of freeing her from a painful relationship, the divorce accelerated Monroe's decline. In February, she confessed thoughts of suicide. She was then committed to Payne Whitney Clinic, the psychiatric ward of a hospital in New York.

Monroe was outraged that those close to her would allow her to be committed. From the moment she arrived at the clinic, Monroe did nothing but try to get out. Many biographies describe her outbursts at the hospital, which include her throwing a chair into a glass door and threatening to kill herself with one of the shards if she was not released. A few days after she was admitted, ex-husband DiMaggio used his celebrity status and a sprinkling of threats aimed at the clinic to get Monroe out. This

▲ RALPH GREENSON CONTINUED TREATING MONROE— AND PROVIDING HER WITH PRESCRIPTION DRUGS—AFTER HER RELEASE FROM THE HOSPITAL.

protective move fueled rumors that the two had rekindled their romance and planned to remarry. However, although DiMaggio obviously cared about his ex-wife, romance was not his first priority at the time. It was clear Monroe was not well. DiMaggio realized she needed help and tried to find a better facility for her. He checked her into another hospital, where she stayed for approximately three weeks. After that, Monroe returned to the care of the eccentric Greenson.

Greenson believed Monroe was suffering from schizophrenia, likely due to the paranoia she had developed and her habit of referring to "Marilyn Monroe" as a character separate from herself.[1]

THE KENNEDYS

In the summer of 1961, as she turned 35, Monroe's mental health remained shaky. She was casually dating famous singer and actor Frank Sinatra. Peter Lawford was a mutual friend of the two. Lawford was married to Pat Kennedy, sister of the recently elected President John F. Kennedy. These people comprised the group of friends who saw Monroe through the final stages of her addiction—and the final year of her life.

Pat introduced Monroe to the president's brother and attorney general, Robert "Bobby" Kennedy, at a dinner party in early 1962. Monroe and Bobby liked each other immediately, and their friendship brought Monroe even closer to the president. Soon after meeting Bobby, Monroe went to another dinner party, held in honor of President Kennedy. Monroe was late as always, which was all the better for making a grand entrance. According to an actress who attended the party that night,

▲ THERE WERE MANY RUMORS CONCERNING THE EXTENT
OF MONROE AND PRESIDENT KENNEDY'S RELATIONSHIP.

*It was magical, really. I've never seen anyone
stop a room like that. The president turned
around and noticed her and you could see that
he was immediately attracted to her.*[2]

The next day, President Kennedy invited
Monroe to accompany him to Palm Springs,

California, where he would be traveling without his wife that March.

Monroe and Kennedy spent the weekend of March 24 together in Palm Springs. Most speculate President Kennedy and Monroe must have become intimate that weekend, though there is no proof of a long-term love affair between them. Whatever happened during that secret-filled weekend, Monroe's close association with the president is a reminder of the power she possessed even as her life was spiraling out of control.

SOMETHING HAD TO GIVE

In April, Monroe began filming *Something's Got to Give,* produced by Fox. It would be her last role. The film, never to be finished, got off to a bad start. Monroe claimed to have fallen ill just before filming was scheduled to begin, setting everything behind. Between late April and mid-May, Monroe was largely absent from the set. However, the few scenes she did film were breathtaking.

Though Fox was happy with her work, the company was bogged down with financial problems at the time and could not afford more delays. Fox executives had originally granted Monroe permission to delay production to perform at President Kennedy's birthday gala in

New York that May. But they now threatened to fire and then sue Monroe if she went. Of course, Monroe went anyway, and her scandalously steamy rendition of "Happy Birthday" became one of the defining moments of her career.

When Monroe returned several days later, Fox executives decided not to follow through on their threats just yet. Monroe was allowed to continue work on *Something's Got to Give*, and she did not hold anything back. In fact, when she was required to do a poolside scene in a flesh-colored bathing suit to appear naked, Monroe took the scene to the next level by actually filming it in the nude. It was the first time a famous US actress had done a nude scene, and it caused a sensation. Images

Fox's Financial Troubles

Much of the financial stress during the filming of *Something's Got to Give* was due to pressure to bail Fox out of a bad situation created by another production, *Cleopatra*. The film starred actress Elizabeth Taylor, who was Monroe's professional rival. Taylor was being paid a salary of $1 million for her role in *Cleopatra*. Parts of the movie were to be filmed in Rome and London, and the costumes and sets were extremely expensive. On top of all this, Taylor became severely ill and progress on the film was stalled for a while, adding to the expenses. When all was said and done, the four-hour movie cost $44 million to make (approximately $300 million in today's dollars). Fox's hope to use Monroe's film to salvage financial damage created by Taylor's would not come to fruition. Instead, the studio would end up with two films disastrous to produce: one grossly expensive, the other unfinished.

of the bare, blonde goddess seated at the edge of a pool appeared on the covers of scores of magazines. It appeared Monroe was back at the top of her game.

As usual, though, Monroe could not sustain her success. Just before her thirty-sixth birthday, she fell back into her old routine. After another flurry of absences, Fox finally made good on its earlier threats. In mid-production in early June, fed up with her breaking her contract and not performing up to par, the studio fired Monroe and sued her for $500,000.

THE LAST SITTING

Monroe felt appalled and betrayed by the termination and lawsuit from Fox. She was determined to show the studio what a big mistake it made by doing a series of glamorous photo shoots. One was what would become an iconic shoot for *Vogue* with photographer Bert Stern. Later called *The Last Sitting*, the shoot took place in late June. Stern captured a nude Monroe in all her beauty and vulnerability, often with no makeup, and her surgical scars displayed proudly. The 2,500 photos Stern took have a haunting quality of sincerity and spontaneity. It is as though Monroe were not posing for them at all but simply caught in a mood of playfulness.

In July, Monroe gave an extended interview for *Life* magazine. She spoke of her fame, her past, her triumphs, and her insecurities.

THE LOST WEEKEND

The last weekend in July 1962, rumors were swirling about Monroe. She was allegedly obsessed with the president and sleeping with his brother, Bobby. Her drug abuse was out of control, but no one seemed aware of exactly how dangerous her behavior had become. Reality set in that weekend when Monroe's occasional date Sinatra invited the Lawfords and Monroe to a resort on the California-Nevada border, where he would be performing.

In addition to the long list of prescription pills and alcohol she was taking, it was discovered Monroe had begun injecting herself with cocktails of drugs. She had also invented ways of getting her prescription drugs into her system faster, such as pricking holes in her pills before

Monroe's Medicine Cabinet

Monroe abused a long list of substances during the last years of her life. The list includes Amytal, antihistamines, Benzedrine, champagne, chloral hydrate, codeine, Demerol, Dexamyl, Dexedrine, gin, Librium, methamphetamines, morphine, Nembutal, Percodan, Phenobarbital, Seconal, sherry, sodium pentothal, sulfathalidine, vermouth, and vodka. These were a mix of narcotics, which relieve pain and dull senses; opiates, which reduce pain and bring on sleep; sedatives, which tranquilize or calm senses; and various types of alcohol.

▲ MONROE IN HER LAST FILM, *SOMETHING'S GOT TO GIVE*, WHICH WAS NEVER COMPLETED

swallowing them. While Monroe's drug use had been common knowledge among friends and on set, her behavior over the weekend, including using the drugs in front of her friends, was a wake-up call on the seriousness of her problem. There are numerous accounts of what happened during that lost weekend, but the common thread seems to be that Monroe was clearly sick, out of control, and possibly close to death.

Although Monroe's personal struggles were at their worst that July, her career appeared headed for an upswing the beginning of August. Her extensive *Life* magazine article ran in the issue published on August 3, 1962. Two days earlier, Fox executives realized they could not finish *Something's Got to Give* without Monroe. They presented her with a new contract, offering her a higher salary and a starring role in at least one other film. It appeared Monroe was looking forward to continuing her work with Fox and was poised to take her career to new heights. But everything would come to an end on the night of August 4, 1962.

———•◆•———

9

AMERICA'S STAR BURNS OUT

Though Monroe's career was on an upswing during the last weeks of her life, her behavior gave friends cause to worry. She overdosed several times, though it is unclear whether the overdoses were accidents, calls for attention, or attempts at suicide. Monroe would phone her friends for help after swallowing a toxic dose of pills, and they would take her to get her stomach pumped. They viewed the incidents as cries for help but never believed Monroe might truly take

▶ MONROE HIT A LOW POINT BY THE SUMMER OF 1962 THAT INCLUDED SUICIDE ATTEMPTS.

her life. According to a private investigator, just after Monroe's death, friend Lawford said,

> *[Monroe] was always threatening suicide. I never took it seriously. You know, she was just blowing off emotional steam. . . . I'll bet there hasn't been a week all summer that she hasn't called me up and swore she was about to take her life.*[1]

AUGUST 4, 1962

Accounts conflict over who Monroe saw and spoke to on the day leading up to her death and whether she was in high or low spirits. Most sources agree Monroe made several phone calls that day. However, so many people have claimed to be on the other end of the line it is nearly impossible to sort out whose numbers she actually dialed. The details of the evening of August 4 are a little more concrete. But the investigation into Monroe's death created enough contradictions, questions, and complexities to prevent any one story from being universally accepted as truth.

The generally accepted account begins early in the evening of August 4, when Lawford called Monroe at her Los Angeles home to invite her to dinner. When she did not show up, he called her again. Monroe said she was tired and wanted to stay home. Her speech was slurred and soft, and it was obvious to Lawford that Monroe had been using drugs. She ended the conversation with: "Say good-bye to Pat, say good-bye to Jack, and say good-bye to yourself, because you're a nice guy."[2] Lawford was concerned. He tried calling Monroe back but got a busy signal and was either not inclined or was convinced not to leave the party to check on her. Instead, he spoke with his agent, who reached Monroe's lawyer, who telephoned Monroe's housekeeper, Eunice Murray. Greenson, who had visited Monroe earlier that night asked Murray to keep an eye on her the remainder of the evening.

When asked over the phone how Monroe was doing, Murray said she was fine, but she did not enter Monroe's bedroom to check on her. The closed bedroom door signified Monroe wanted to be left alone, and Murray did not wish to disturb her. Murray allegedly did not become alarmed until the

The Official Statement

The official statement on Monroe's death read: "On more than one occasion in the past, when disappointed and depressed, [Monroe] had made a suicide attempt using sedative drugs. On these occasions, she had called for help and had been rescued. From the information collected about the events of August 4, it is our opinion that the same pattern was repeated except for the rescue."[3]

early hours of August 5, when Monroe's bedroom light was still on, the door was locked, and Murray could get no response from Monroe. Murray went outside to get a glimpse of Monroe through her bedroom window, and saw the star sprawled on her bed in an odd position. Murray immediately called Greenson, who broke in through the window to find Monroe dead. From the open pill bottles on her nightstand, it was apparent Monroe had either accidentally or deliberately overdosed. Greenson phoned another of Monroe's doctors, who agreed with Greenson about the cause of death being an overdose. Only after all this did anyone call the police. The police department reported it finally received notification that Monroe was dead around 4:30 a.m. on August 5, 1962. She was 36 years old. Later that day, the world would be shocked by the news.

INVESTIGATIONS AND CONSPIRACIES

The official investigation and autopsy report revealed Monroe died of an overdose of drugs including Nembutal and chloral hydrate, both used for short-term relief from insomnia or to reduce a patient's anxiety and help him or her sleep before surgery. The verdict was probable suicide. However, many were unsatisfied with this explanation. Some argued Monroe had seemed happy about her recent successes and had no reason to want to end her life. People came up with many unlikely stories of assassination plots and cover-up operations. None of these theories was ever proven credible but instead seem the result of a grieving public grasping for a reason behind its beloved star's death.

Government investigations of Monroe prior to her death sound at first like an aspect of a wild theory but are grounded in truth. Due to Monroe's association with Miller, who was still being investigated by the HUAC, as well as Monroe's connection with the Kennedy family, her phones were wiretapped. It is unclear whether Monroe was aware

A Final Farewell

Monroe's funeral took place on the afternoon of August 8, 1962. It was a small gathering of 31 close family members and friends, including second husband DiMaggio. First and third husbands Dougherty and Miller did not attend.

Monroe's body was displayed in an open casket. She was dressed in a favorite green gown, and her makeup artist made sure she looked the way her loved ones would want to remember her. Close friend Strasberg gave a touching eulogy in which he tried to describe Monroe's special appeal:

She had a luminous quality—a combination of wistfulness, radiance, yearning—to set her apart and yet make everyone wish to be a part of it, to share in the childish naïveté which was at once so shy and yet so vibrant.[4]

of her phones being wiretapped, but some sources suggest she had suspicions. Transcripts of tape recordings Monroe allegedly made for Greenson were published and proof to some that Monroe had not committed suicide, casting further doubt on the initial investigation. All of the theories, rumors, and contradictions led to a second FBI investigation in 1982. This investigation confirmed the original assessment, though as coroner Thomas Noguchi noted,

> *No one will ever be able to say definitely what went on that evening which . . . transformed Marilyn Monroe from a beautiful and talented actress . . . to a dying movie star—and an undying legend.*[5]

LEGACY

The mystique surrounding Monroe has continued to fascinate for more than half a century. Monroe remains an icon of glamour, beauty, sexuality, and femininity. Countless photographers, biographers, filmmakers, and artists have posthumously immortalized her. It seems the same combination of beauty,

Lost Love

Like the rest of the world, DiMaggio was shocked at the news of Monroe's death. DiMaggio arranged the funeral, keeping it private for family and close friends. For two decades afterward, he delivered flowers to her grave twice a week.

▲ MONROE REMAINS AN OBJECT OF GLAMOUR AND INTRIGUE AND A MUSE TO MANY ARTISTS, IMPERSONATORS, AND PERFORMERS.

tragedy, talent, and mystery that made so many fall in love with Monroe will keep her memory alive for generations to come.

TIMELINE

1926

1935

1942

Norma Jean Mortenson is born on June 1 to Gladys Baker and an unknown father.

On September 13, Norma Jean is placed in the Los Angeles Orphans' Home.

Norma Jean marries Jim Dougherty on June 19.

1950

1951

1952

Monroe appears in *The Asphalt Jungle* and *All About Eve*, the films that launch her career.

In the spring, Monroe signs another contract with Fox.

Monroe has her first date with Joe DiMaggio early in the year.

1945

In August, Norma Jean signs with Emmeline Snively's Blue Book Modeling Agency.

1946

Norma Jean signs her first contract with Twentieth Century Fox in August and changes her name to Marilyn Monroe.

1948

In March, Monroe signs a contract with Columbia Pictures.

1952

Monroe has her first starring roles in *Niagara* and *Gentlemen Prefer Blondes.*

1953

Monroe films *How to Marry a Millionaire* and *River of No Return.*

1954

On January 14, Monroe marries DiMaggio.

IMELINE

1954

Monroe files for divorce from DiMaggio in October following the filming of *The Seven Year Itch.*

1954

In December, Monroe leaves Fox, moves to New York, and establishes Marilyn Monroe Productions with Milton Greene.

1955

Monroe re-signs with Fox in December.

1962

In March, Monroe spends the weekend with President Kennedy in Palm Springs, California.

1962

Monroe begins filming *Something's Got to Give* in April.

1962

On May 19, Monroe sings "Happy Birthday" at President Kennedy's birthday gala.

1956

Monroe weds third husband Arthur Miller in June.

1960

Monroe films *The Misfits* with Clark Gable. The script is written by Arthur Miller.

1961

In January, Monroe divorces Miller.

1962

In late June, Monroe poses for photographs for *Vogue* taken by Ben Stern. This session will later be called *The Last Sitting*.

1962

Monroe is found dead on the morning of August 5. The investigation reveals it to be a probable suicide.

1962

A funeral is held for Monroe on August 8.

QUICK FACTS

DATE OF BIRTH
June 1, 1926

PLACE OF BIRTH
Los Angeles, California

DATE OF DEATH
August 5, 1962

PLACE OF DEATH
Los Angeles, California

PARENTS
Gladys Baker and unknown father

MARRIAGES
Jim Dougherty (1942–1946)
Joe DiMaggio (1954)
Arthur Miller (1956–1961)

CAREER HIGHLIGHTS

Selected Films

Scudda Hoo! Scudda Hay! (1948)
Ladies of the Chorus (1948)
Love Happy (1949)
The Asphalt Jungle (1950)
All About Eve (1950)
Clash by Night (1952)
Don't Bother to Knock (1952)
Monkey Business (1952)
Niagara (1953)
Gentlemen Prefer Blondes (1953)
How to Marry a Millionaire (1953)
River of No Return (1954)
There's No Business Like Show Business (1954)
The Seven Year Itch (1955)
Bus Stop (1956)
The Prince and the Showgirl (1957)
Some Like It Hot (1959)
Let's Make Love (1960)
The Misfits (1961)
Something's Got to Give (unfinished)

QUOTE

"I believed in myself. I just had to make it. I was determined to make it. Nothing was going to get in my way." —*Marilyn Monroe*

GLOSSARY

agent
> A business representative who is authorized to act on behalf of his or her client.

columnist
> A person who writes a regular series of newspaper or magazine articles.

Communist
> A person associated with an economic and political system in which the government, or state, controls the economy.

coyly
> Marked by artful playfulness.

diva
> A person who has a difficult time working under direction or as a part of a team because he or she is vain or undisciplined.

electrolysis
> The destruction of hair roots by using an electric current.

icon
> An object of devotion; a symbol.

mystique
> An air or attitude of mystery and reverence developing around something or someone.

posthumously
  Happening or continuing after a person dies.

predecessor
  A person who held a position before another succeeded him or her.

psychoanalyst
  A doctor who examines a person's mind and tries to discover the unconscious sources of mental and emotional disorders.

scandal
  Damage to or loss of reputation from public disclosure of improper circumstance or action.

schizophrenia
  A mental disorder characterized by loss of touch with reality and disturbances in thoughts, perceptions, and behaviors.

screen test
  A short, filmed test to determine an actor's ability for a movie role.

starlet
  A young actress who aspires to become a star and is coached and publicized for starring roles.

voluptuous
  Having an attractive, curvaceous form that suggests sensual pleasure.

ADDITIONAL RESOURCES

SELECTED BIBLIOGRAPHY

Barris, George. *Marilyn—Her Life In Her Own Words: Marilyn Monroe's Revealing Last Words and Photographs.* Secaucus, NJ: Carol, 1995. Print.

Charyn, Jerome. *Marilyn: The Last Goddess.* New York: Abrams, 2008. Print.

"Marilyn Lets Her Hair Down about Being Famous." *Life* 3 Aug. 1962: 37. Print.

Shwarz, Ted. *Marilyn Revealed: The Ambitious Life of an American Icon.* Lanham, MD: Taylor Trade, 2009. Print.

Taraborrelli, Randy J. *The Secret Life of Marilyn Monroe.* New York: Grand Central, 2009. Print.

FURTHER READINGS

Banner, Lois W. *MM–Personal: From the Private Archive of Marilyn Monroe.* New York: Abrams, 2010. Print.

Buchthal, Stanley, and Bernard Comment, eds. *Fragments: Poems, Intimate Notes, Letters by Marilyn Monroe.* New York: Farrar, Straus and Giroux, 2010. Print.

Monroe, Marilyn. *My Story.* New York: Cooper Square, 2000. Print.

Stern, Bert. *The Last Sitting.* New York: Random House, 2007. Print.

WEB LINKS

To learn more about Marilyn Monroe, visit ABDO Publishing
Company online at **www.abdopublishing.com**. Web sites
about Marilyn Monroe are featured on our Book Links page.
These links are routinely monitored and updated to provide the
most current information available.

FOR MORE INFORMATION

For more information on this subject, contact or visit the
following organizations.

Grauman's Chinese Theatre
6801 Hollywood Boulevard, Hollywood, CA 90028
323-461-3331
www.chinesetheatres.com
The handprints and footprints of Hollywood stars, including
those of Marilyn Monroe, are forever preserved in concrete in
front of Grauman's Chinese Theatre.

Marilyn Monroe's Grave
Westwood Village Memorial Park Cemetery
1218 Glendon Avenue, Westwood, CA 90024
Marilyn Monroe's crypt lies in a small cemetery in Westwood,
California, which is also the burial place of many other
Hollywood stars.

***The Seven Year Itch* Subway Scene Location**
Corner of Lexington Avenue and 52nd Street
New York, NY 10022
Fans of Monroe can stand over the subway grate where she
filmed her most famous scene from *The Seven Year Itch*.

SOURCE NOTES

Chapter 1. Better than Birthday Cake

1. "Marilyn Monroe: Happy Birthday Mr. President." *YouTube.* YouTube, 26 Nov. 2007. Web. 30 Nov. 2011.

2. Randy J. Taraborrelli. *The Secret Life of Marilyn Monroe.* New York: Grand Central, 2009. Print. 433.

3. "Marilyn Lets Her Hair Down about Being Famous." *Life* 3 Aug. 1962: 37. *Google Book Search.* Web. 10 May 2012.

4. Ibid.

5. "Marilyn Monroe: Happy Birthday Mr. President." *YouTube.* YouTube, 26 Nov. 2007. Web. 30 Nov. 2011.

Chapter 2. The Early Life of Norma Jean

1. George Barris. *Marilyn—Her Life In Her Own Words: Marilyn Monroe's Revealing Last Words and Photographs.* Secaucus, NJ: Carol, 1995. Print. 15.

2. Jerome Charyn. *Marilyn: The Last Goddess.* New York: Abrams, 2008. Print. 22.

3. Randy J. Taraborrelli. *The Secret Life of Marilyn Monroe.* New York: Grand Central, 2009. Print. 72.

Chapter 3. An Ambitious Beauty

1. Jerome Charyn. *Marilyn: The Last Goddess.* New York: Abrams, 2008. Print. 23–24.

2. Ibid. 24.

3. George Barris. *Marilyn—Her Life In Her Own Words: Marilyn Monroe's Revealing Last Words and Photographs.* Secaucus, NJ: Carol Publishing Group, 1995. *Google Book Search.* Web. 10 May 2012.

4. Ted Shwarz. *Marilyn Revealed: The Ambitious Life of an American Icon.* Lanham, MD: Taylor Trade, 2009. Print. 132.

5. Ibid. 174.

6. Randy J. Taraborrelli. *The Secret Life of Marilyn Monroe.* New York: Grand Central, 2009. Print. 114.

Chapter 4. The Making of Marilyn Monroe

1. Randy J. Taraborrelli. *The Secret Life of Marilyn Monroe.* New York: Grand Central, 2009. Print. 134.

2. Ted Shwarz. *Marilyn Revealed: The Ambitious Life of an American Icon.* Lanham, MD: Taylor Trade, 2009. Print. 239.

3. Jerome Charyn. *Marilyn: The Last Goddess.* New York: Abrams, 2008. Print. 25.

4. "The Legend of Marilyn Monroe." *YouTube.* YouTube, 25 June 2009. Web. 10 May 2012.

5. Joseph L. Mankiewicz and Brian Dauth, eds. *Joseph L. Mankiewicz: Interviews.* UP of Mississippi, 2008. *Google Book Search.* Web. 10 May 2012.

Chapter 5. The Brightest Star

1. Ted Shwarz. *Marilyn Revealed: The Ambitious Life of an American Icon.* Lanham, MD: Taylor Trade, 2009. Print. 254.

2. Randy J. Taraborrelli. *The Secret Life of Marilyn Monroe.* New York: Grand Central, 2009. Print. 222.

Chapter 6. In and Out of Control

1. Bosley Crowther. "There's No Business Like Show Business (1954)." *New York Times.* New York Times, 17 Dec. 1954. Web. 20 Dec. 2011.

2. Randy J. Taraborrelli. *The Secret Life of Marilyn Monroe.* New York: Grand Central, 2009. Print. 241.

3. Ibid. 245.

Chapter 7. New Depths

1. Ted Shwarz. *Marilyn Revealed: The Ambitious Life of an American Icon.* Lanham, MD: Taylor Trade, 2009. Print. 506.

SOURCE NOTES

CONTINUED

2. Randy J. Taraborrelli. *The Secret Life of Marilyn Monroe.* New York: Grand Central, 2009. Print. 303.

3. Ted Shwarz. *Marilyn Revealed: The Ambitious Life of an American Icon.* Lanham, MD: Taylor Trade, 2009. Print. 542.

Chapter 8. The Final Years

1. Ted Shwarz. *Marilyn Revealed: The Ambitious Life of an American Icon.* Lanham, MD: Taylor Trade, 2009. Print. 581.

2. Randy J. Taraborrelli. *The Secret Life of Marilyn Monroe.* New York: Grand Central, 2009. Print. 406.

Chapter 9. America's Star Burns Out

1. Ted Shwarz. *Marilyn Revealed: The Ambitious Life of an American Icon.* Lanham, MD: Taylor Trade, 2009. Print. 625.

2. Ibid. 619.

3. Ibid. 622.

4. Stanley Buchthal and Bernard Comment, eds. *Fragments: Poems, Intimate Notes, Letters by Marilyn Monroe.* New York: Farrar, Straus and Giroux, 2010. Print. 231.

5. Ted Shwarz. *Marilyn Revealed: The Ambitious Life of an American Icon.* Lanham, MD: Taylor Trade, 2009. Print. 648.

INDEX

INDEX

CONTINUED

ABOUT THE AUTHOR

Lisa Owings has a degree in English and creative writing from the University of Minnesota. She has written and edited a wide variety of educational books for children. Owings lives in Andover, Minnesota, with her husband.

PHOTO CREDITS

Michael Ochs Archives/Getty Images, cover, 3, 45, 64, 67; 20th Century-Fox Film Corp/Everett Collection, 7, 51, 53, 89; 5356/Gamma-Rapho via Getty Images, 9, 98 (bottom); Everett Collection, 13, 33, 39, 72, 96 (bottom); AP Images, 15, 47, 55, 70, 75, 79, 81, 97 (bottom), 99 (top); Silver Screen Collection/Hulton Archive/Getty Images, 18, 23, 27; Mondadori/Getty Images, 25, 96 (top); Joseph Jasgur/Julien's Auctions/File/AP Images, 30, 97 (top); Frank Driggs Collection/Archive Photos/Getty Images, 35; Bettmann/Corbis/AP Images, 43; Dave Cicero/Bettmann/Corbis/AP Images, 57; Rex Features/AP Images, 60, 98 (top); Moviestore Collection/Rex/Rex USA, 86; Massimo Sambucetti/AP Images, 95